# HOUGHTON MIFFLIN

# Try to See It My Way

**Senior Authors**

J. David Cooper
John J. Pikulski

**Authors**

Kathryn H. Au
Margarita Calderón
Jacqueline C. Comas
Marjorie Y. Lipson
J. Sabrina Mims
Susan E. Page
Sheila W. Valencia
MaryEllen Vogt

**Consultants**

Dolores Malcolm
Tina Saldivar
Shane Templeton

Acknowledgments appear on page Acknowledgments 1 at the back of this book.

Printed in the U.S.A.          ISBN: 0-395-76269-3          123456789-WC-98 97 96 95

## INVITATIONS TO LITERACY

# Houghton Mifflin Company • Boston
**Atlanta • Dallas • Geneva, Illinois • Palo Alto • Princeton**

Try to See It My Way

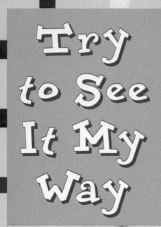

# Try to See It My Way

# CONTENTS

THE
HUNDRED PENNY BOX

SHARON BELL MATHIS
Illustrated by Leo & Diane Dillon

PAPERBACK **PLUS**

### The Hundred Penny Box

*by Sharon Bell Mathis*

In a box of one hundred pennies,
Michael's great-great-aunt, Aunt Dew,
keeps the stories of her one hundred
years.

### In the same book . . .

More about Aunt Dew's family tree,
pennies through history, and another
seasoned storyteller

**PAPERBACK PLUS**

## Dear Mr. Henshaw

*by Beverly Cleary*

Leigh Botts writes to his favorite author . . . and finds out about himself.

### In the same book . . .

Much more, including Beverly Cleary and her readers, trucks, and monarch butterflies

### Hello, My Name Is Scrambled Eggs

*by Jamie Gilson*
Will Tuan Nguyen, newly arrived from Vietnam, be Americanized by his American friend?

### A Llama in the Family

*by Johanna Hurwitz*
Instead of the mountain bike Adam is hoping for, his mother buys a llama to start a new business.

### Stealing Home

*by Mary Stolz*
When his great-aunt visits, Thomas is afraid that his life of fishing and base-ball with his grandfather will change.

### The Facts and Fictions of Minna Pratt

*by Patricia MacLachlan*
Minna wishes that her mother, a writer, and her father, a psychologist, would act normal, like the parents of her friends.

### In Two Worlds: A Yup'ik Eskimo Family

*by Aylette Jenness*
An Eskimo family tries to observe its ancient customs while living in a world of modern conveniences.

### Red-Dirt Jessie

*by Anna Myers*
Jessie is sure that taming a half-wild dog as a pet will cheer up her father.

# Meet the Author of
# In the Year of the Boar and Jackie Robinson

## Bette Bao Lord

At age 10

The story of Shirley Temple Wong's arrival in America from China is based on Bette Bao Lord's own childhood. She remembers sailing into San Francisco in the autumn of 1946: "Only yesterday, resting my chin on the rails of the S.S. *Marylinx,* I peered into the mist for *Mei Guo,* beautiful country. It refused to appear. Then, within a blink, there was the Golden Gate, more like the portals to heaven than the arches of a man-made bridge." From California the family made its way to New York.

"I arrived in Brooklyn, New York, on a Sunday," she recalls. "On Monday I was enrolled at P. S. 8. By putting up ten fingers, I found myself sentenced to the fifth grade. It was a terrible mistake. By American reckoning, I had just turned eight. And so I was the shortest student by a head or two in class."

Like Shirley, Lord persevered and learned English. For a short time, she dreamed of winning a Nobel Prize in chemistry. But she went on to a career helping to promote understanding between China and the United States, and for several years she taught and performed modern dance.

Lord "stumbled into writing" by deciding to tell the story of her sister Sansan, "who grew up in China [and] was reunited with the family after a separation of sixteen years." Much later she wrote about her own early life in the United States. The result was her first book for children, *In the Year of the Boar and Jackie Robinson,* in which "China's Little Ambassador" is a chapter.

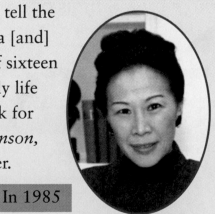

In 1985

# Meet the Illustrator

Drawing the illustrations for *In the Year of the Boar and Jackie Robinson* brought back a lot of memories for Winson Trang. Like Shirley, the heroine of the story, Trang was born in Asia and came to the United States knowing no English. Trang arrived in San Francisco in 1979 when he was 15 years old.

Trang had to travel a long and dangerous route to get to the United States. He left his homeland, Vietnam, in 1975 at the end of a long war. With a cousin, he traveled by train to China, the country where his grandparents were born. Then he traveled by boat to Hong Kong, where he lived in a refugee camp for a year before relatives helped him gain passage to the United States.

Other members of Trang's family reached the United States by different routes, sometimes narrowly avoiding disaster. His mother and sisters were on a boat that capsized. Out of a total of four hundred passengers, they were among the ninety who survived.

Trang learned English quickly and, after college, attended art school. Working as a translator of Chinese, he began to find work as a freelance illustrator. One of his assignments was *Child of the Owl*, by Lawrence Yep.

Trang offers his own story as encouragement to young people interested in a career as an illustrator. "Keep at it," he says. "Hang on until you get your opportunity!"

*In China her family calls her Sixth Cousin or sometimes Bandit. But just before Bandit and her mother sail to America to join her father, she changes her name to Shirley Temple Wong. The time of her arrival is 1947. In China it's the Year of the Boar. The place is Brooklyn, New York. And Shirley is about to face a major challenge: her first day in an American school.*

# China's Little Ambassador

Nine o'clock sharp the very next morning, Shirley sat in the principal's office at P. S. 8. Her mother and the schoolmistress were talking. Shirley didn't understand a word. It was embarrassing. Why hadn't she, too, studied the English course on the records that Father had sent? But it was too late now. She stopped trying to understand. Suddenly, Mother hissed, in Chinese. "Stop that or else!"

Shirley snapped her head down. She had been staring at the stranger. But she could not keep her eyes from rolling up again. There was something more foreign about the principal than about any other foreigner she had seen so far. What was it?

# In the Year of the Boar and Jackie Robinson

*by Bette Bao Lord*

It was not the blue eyes. Many others had them too. It was not the high nose. All foreign noses were higher than Chinese ones. It was not the blue hair. Hair came in all colors in America.

Yes, of course, naturally. The woman had no eyelashes. Other foreigners grew hair all over them, more than six Chinese together. This woman had none. Her skin was as bare as the Happy Buddha's belly, except for the neat rows of stiff curls that hugged her head.

She had no eyebrows, even. They were penciled on, and looked just like the character for man, 人. And every time she tilted her head, her hair moved all in one piece like a hat.

"Shirley."

Mother was trying to get her attention. "Tell the principal how old you are."

Shirley put up ten fingers.

While the principal filled out a form, Mother argued excitedly. But why? Shirley had given the correct answer. She counted just to make sure. On the day she was born, she was one year old. And two months later, upon the new year, she was two. That was the Year of the Rabbit. Then came the Dragon, Snake, Horse, Sheep, Monkey, Rooster, Dog and now it was the year of the Boar, making ten. Proof she was ten.

Mother shook her head. Apparently, she had lost the argument. She announced in Chinese, "Shirley, you will enter fifth grade."

"Fifth? But, Mother, I don't speak English. And besides, I only completed three grades in Chungking."

"I know. But the principal has explained that in America everyone is assigned according to age. Ten years old means fifth grade. And we must observe the American rules, mustn't we?"

Shirley nodded obediently. But she could not help thinking that only Shirley had to go to school, and only Shirley would be in trouble if she failed.

Mother stood up to leave. She took Shirley by the hand. "Remember, my daughter, you may be the only Chinese these Americans will ever meet. Do your best. Be extra good. Upon your shoulders rests the reputation of all Chinese."

All five hundred million? Shirley wondered.

"You are China's little ambassador."

"Yes, Mother." Shirley squared her shoulders and tried to feel worthy of this great honor. At the same time she wished she could leave with Mother.

Alone, the schoolmistress and Shirley looked at each other. Suddenly the principal shut one eye, the right one, then opened it again.

Was this another foreign custom, like shaking hands? It must be proper if a principal does it, Shirley thought. She ought to return the gesture, but she didn't know how. So she shut and opened both eyes. Twice.

This brought a warm laugh.

226

The principal then led her to class. The room was large, with windows up to the ceiling. Row after row of students, each one unlike the next. Some faces were white, like clean plates; others black like ebony. Some were in-between shades. A few were spotted all over. One boy was as big around as a water jar. Several others were as thin as chopsticks. No one wore a uniform of blue, like hers. There were sweaters with animals on them, shirts with stripes and shirts with squares, dresses in colors as varied as Grand-grand Uncle's paints. Three girls even wore earrings.

While Shirley looked about, the principal had been making a speech. Suddenly it ended with "Shirley Temple Wong." The class stood up and waved.

*Amitabha!* They were all so tall. Even Water Jar was a head taller than she. For a fleeting moment she wondered if Mother would consider buying an ambassador a pair of high-heeled shoes.

"Hi, Shirley!" The class shouted.

Shirley bowed deeply. Then, taking a guess, she replied, "Hi!"

The teacher introduced herself and showed the new pupil to a front-row seat. Shirley liked her right away, although she had a most difficult name, Mrs. Rappaport. She was a tiny woman with dainty bones and fiery red hair brushed skyward. Shirley thought that in her previous life she must have been a bird, a cardinal perhaps. Yet she commanded respect, for no student

228

talked out of turn. Or was it the long mean pole that hung on the wall behind the desk that commanded respect? It dwarfed the bamboo cane the teacher in Chungking had used to punish Four Hands whenever he stole a trifle from another.

Throughout the lessons, Shirley leaned forward, barely touching her seat, to catch the meaning, but the words sounded like gurgling water. Now and then, when Mrs. Rappaport looked her way, she opened and shut her eyes as the principal had done, to show friendship.

At lunchtime, Shirley went with the class to the school cafeteria, but before she could pick up a tray, several boys and girls waved for her to follow them. They were smiling, so she went along. They snuck back to the classroom to pick up coats, then hurried out the door and across the school yard to a nearby store. Shirley was certain they should not be there, but what choice did she have? These were now her friends.

One by one they gave their lunch money to the store owner, whom they called "Mr. P." In return, he gave each a bottle of orange-colored water, bread twice the size of an ear of corn oozing with meat balls, peppers, onions, and hot red gravy, and a large piece of brown paper to lay on the icy sidewalk and sit upon. While they ate, everyone except Shirley played marbles or cards and traded bottle caps and pictures of men swinging a stick or wearing one huge glove. It was the best lunch Shirley had ever had.

And there was more. After lunch, each of them was allowed to select one item from those displayed under the glass counter. There were paper strips dotted with red and yellow sugar tacks, chocolate soldiers in blue tin foil, boxes of raisins and nuts, envelopes of chips, cookies as big as pancakes, candy elephants, lollipops in every color, a wax collection of red lips, white teeth, pink ears and curly black mustaches. Shirley was the last to make up her mind. She chose a hand, filled with juice. It looked better than it tasted, but she did not mind. Tomorrow she could choose again.

But when she was back in her seat, waiting for Mrs. Rappaport to enter the classroom, Shirley's knees shook. What if the teacher found out about her escapade? There would go her ambassadorship. She would be shamed. Her parents would lose face. All five hundred million Chinese would suffer. Round and round in her stomach the meat balls tumbled like pebbles.

Then Mrs. Rappaport came in. She did not look pleased. Shirley flinched when the teacher went straight to the long mean pole. For the first time her heart went out to Four Hands. She shut her eyes and prayed to the Goddess of Mercy. Oh Kwan Yin, please don't let me cry! She waited, listening for Mrs. Rappaport's footsteps to become louder and louder. They did not. Finally curiosity overcame fear and she looked up. Mrs. Rappaport was using the pole to open a window!

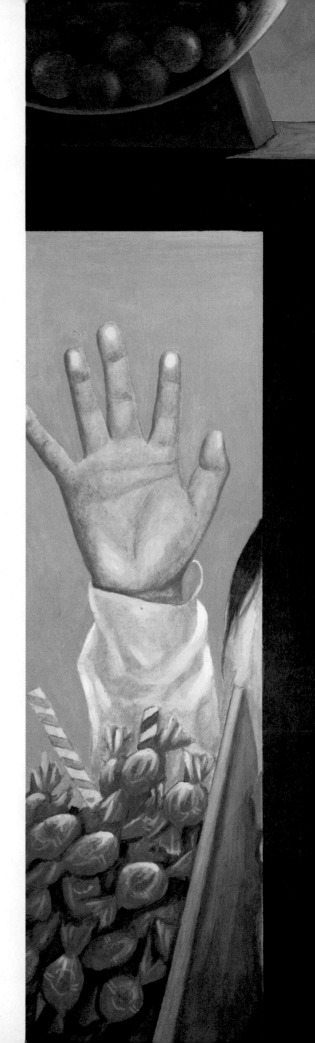

232

233

The lessons continued. During arithmetic, Shirley raised her hand. She went to the blackboard and wrote the correct answer. Mrs. Rappaport rewarded her with a big smile. Shirley opened and shut her eyes to show her pleasure. Soon, she was dreaming about candy elephants and cookies the size of pancakes.

Then school was over. As Shirley was putting on her coat, Mrs. Rappaport handed her a letter, obviously to be given to her parents. Fear returned. Round and round, this time like rocks.

She barely greeted her mother at the door.

"What happened?"

"Nothing."

"You look sick."

"I'm all right."

"Perhaps it was something you ate at lunch?"

"No," she said much too quickly. "Nothing at all to do with lunch."

"What then?"

"The job of ambassador is harder than I thought."

At bedtime, Shirley could no longer put off giving up the letter. Trembling, she handed it to Father. She imagined herself on a boat back to China.

He read it aloud to Mother. Then they both turned to her, a most quizzical look on their faces.

"Your teacher suggests we take you to a doctor. She thinks there is something wrong with your eyes."

234

# See It Shirley's

## Draw a Picture

### In a Class by Herself

Think about Shirley's classroom on her first day of school. Which people and objects stand out? Draw a picture of Shirley's classroom as Shirley sees it.

## Write a Letter

### Dear Fourth Cousin

How would Shirley describe her first day of school to her favorite cousin back in China? Write a letter that Shirley might write, telling how she feels about being in America.

SCIENCE CIENCIA

Way

## Write a Guide

### *What a Wink Means*

Strange poles, unusual food, people shutting and opening their eyes . . . Shirley is surrounded by hundreds of new details. Write a guidebook for Shirley, explaining some of the items and customs of her school and classroom.

## Compare and Contrast

### *In the Same Boat*

Think about a time when you were a newcomer in a group. How did you feel? What did you notice? Have a discussion comparing your "new kid" experience with Shirley's.

# My Cat, Kuro

## A Description by Mark Aoyama

To someone else, Kuro might look like any other black cat. But to Mark, Kuro is very special indeed. Mark wrote this description to help other people "see" Kuro as he does.

**Mark Aoyama**
North Beach Elementary School
Seattle, Washington

Mark was in the fifth grade when he wrote this description of his special cat. In addition to writing, Mark likes to read, play soccer, draw, make things, and play video games. Someday Mark would like to be an artist or a designer of video games.

# My Cat, Kuro

My cat, Kuro, which is Japanese for "Blackie," is part Persian and part Siamese. Anyway, that's what we think. He is as black and as shiny as polished obsidian. And he is as big as a French poodle. When he lies on our kitchen floor, he stretches out like a bungee cord until he reaches three-and-one-half feet from the tip of his front paws to the tip of his back paws.

Kuro did not always look like a beautiful fur scarf. He came to live with us when my mom found him wandering around where she works. He had no collar and no place to live. When she brought him home, he was dirty and had fleas and ringworm fungus. He only weighed nine pounds, and his ribs poked out from his sides. Now he is round and sleek, weighing in at fourteen pounds, four ounces.

There are lots of ways Kuro communicates with us by making different sounds. When he needs to go outside or wants food, he makes a loud, hollow "Mroowuu." But, when you're

holding the container of catnip, he makes a high-pitched, pleading, three-syllabled "Merow-erow-erow." When Kuro wants to come in from outside, he rubs his paws against the kitchen window, making a squeaking noise on the glass. He always says "hello" as he comes through the door, a sweet little chirplike "Brrrip."

Kuro has yellowish-green eyes, but he can only see out of one of them because of a congenital cataract. This doesn't keep him from catching a large assortment of birds, rats, and mice. Kuro is very proud of these "presents," which he leaves for us. He must feel as if he has caught dinner for our family.

Except when catching little furry things, Kuro is lazy. Most of his day is spent sleeping, eating, sleeping, watching television, sleeping, looking out the window, sleeping, and sitting under the bushes.

I like to nuzzle Kuro's soft, thick fur. That's how I know where he's been last. If he smells like clean air, he's been running or lying down in the open. If he smells like wet dirt, he has been sleeping under the rhododendron bushes. But sometimes he smells perfumy like laundry detergent. Then I know that he has been sleeping in the clean laundry. One day Kuro was sleeping in the black laundry when my mom walked by the laundry basket. He greeted my mom with his "Brrrip," and he scared my mom half to death because she didn't even know he was there. She thought the laundry was alive.

My cat has a superfriendly personality. Although he shows no mercy to rodents, he is very loving to our family members. Kuro will jump into my mother's arms from the floor when he wants to be held.

If my mom hadn't brought Kuro home when he was a stray, he probably wouldn't be alive now. I love Kuro, and I can't imagine what the world would be like without him.

241

# HOANG ANH
## A VIETNAMESE-AMERICAN BOY

BY DIANE HOYT-GOLDSMITH / PHOTOGRAPHS BY LAWRENCE MIGDALE

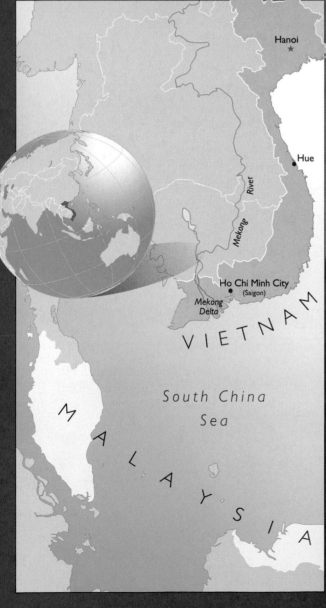

Vietnam is located on the eastern side of the Indochinese Peninsula, in Southeast Asia. In 1978 Hoang Anh's family fled Vietnam. They first went to Malaysia, which lies to the south-west of Vietnam, across the South China Sea.

242

# Hoang Anh

## A Vietnamese-American Boy

by Diane Hoyt-Goldsmith

My name is Hoang Anh Chau (*WONG ON CHOH*). I live in the town of San Rafael, California. In our home, we speak two languages: Vietnamese and English. I came to this country with my family when I was just a baby. We are all refugees from Vietnam, here to begin a new life. My parents, my older brothers, my sister, and I are new citizens of the United States. We are Vietnamese-Americans.

My father, Thao Chau (*TAU CHOH*), is a fisherman. On days when the weather is good, he gets up at three o'clock in the morning. He goes to his boat and heads out to the ocean. Working hard all day, my father visits the places where he has set traps to catch crabs and eels. Usually, he doesn't get home until long after dark. My father learned to be a fisherman in Vietnam.

Hoang Anh's father raises the wire crab trap with a winch and cable that is powered by electricity. The white plastic cup in the center holds the bait.

Happy that the morning's catch was good, Hoang Anh helps his father put the crabs into a tall barrel. His father will take the crabs to a fish market in San Francisco, where they will be sold.

My parents came from a small town called Kieng Giang *(KEENG JANG)* on the Mekong *(MAY-KONG)* Delta in the southern part of Vietnam. In that region, there are many rice farms. My father, like his father before him, owned a tractor and earned a living by plowing the fields for farmers.

But in 1977, my parents made a decision that changed their lives. They decided to leave Vietnam.

My father had been a soldier in the South Vietnamese army since 1971. For years, he had fought alongside the Americans against the Communist forces led by North Vietnam. During the war, many of my father's friends and relatives were killed. He watched as the war destroyed homes, farms, and towns. He saw that his way of life was changing forever.

Unable to defeat the Communists, the United States sent its soldiers home in 1973. Two years later, the Communists of North Vietnam took control of the entire country. The new government acted harshly toward people like my father who had fought against them. My parents were frightened for their own safety. They worried about the future. They wanted to raise their children in a better place.

The Communist government of Vietnam, however, would not allow people to leave the country. So my parents planned secretly to escape from Vietnam and seek a new life of safety and freedom in the United States. In doing so, they would become refugees.

To carry out his plan, my father sold his tractor and bought a small fishing boat. He learned to fish, working in the waters of the Gulf of Thailand. He had a plan to escape, but he did not want the Vietnamese government to become suspicious. He watched and waited for the right time.

Then one day in 1978, my parents gathered together some food and clothing for a long journey. They said goodbye to their parents and their friends. In the dark of the night, my parents brought their four young children on board the small fishing boat. With his family and twenty-four other refugees hidden below the deck, my father sailed away from the shores of Vietnam.

He pretended it was just another day of fishing. But when the little boat reached the open water, he did not stop to put out the crab traps. Sailing west and south, he kept on going toward the island nation of Malaysia.

My brothers and sister were much too young to
realize what was happening. They had no idea of
the danger they were in. The small, overcrowded boat
faced many hardships on the journey. It could have
been lost at sea. It could have been swamped in a
terrible storm. The passengers could have run out of
food and water before reaching land again. Worst of
all, sea pirates could have discovered the boat and
taken everybody's belongings and even their lives.

But my family was lucky. After two days and two
nights on the ocean, they reached Malaysia safely.
For more than a year, they lived in a camp for refugees.
It was filled with many other people who had fled
from Vietnam. Conditions in the
camp were very poor. There was
little food to eat and nothing for
people to do.

It was in this refugee camp
in Malaysia that I was born. In
spite of the poor conditions there,
I was a very healthy baby. When I
was a few months old, a church in
Oregon sponsored my family, and
we emigrated to the United States.

I have read in books that over
a million people fled from Vietnam after the war because they
were frightened about what the
country would be like under a
Communist government. Many
of these "boat people" made it to
safety, as my family did. But many

246

more were shipwrecked and had to be rescued by passing boats. Some were discovered by the Communist government and sent back to Vietnam. The most unfortunate people were those who met pirate ships. They were robbed, beaten, kidnapped, sold as slaves, or even tossed overboard. As a result many refugees have just disappeared completely.

Sometimes, when I help my father at the docks, I look at his fishing boat and think about his daring escape. The boat that carried my family away from Vietnam was ten feet shorter in length, yet it brought thirty people to a new life. My parents were very brave to have taken such risks to bring us all to the United States.

Hoang Anh's father fishes from this boat. It is much larger than the boat that brought his family and many other refugees out of Vietnam.

# Ma! Don't Throw That Shirt Out

## by Jack Prelutsky

Ma!  Don't throw that shirt out,
it's my all-time favorite shirt!
I admit it smells peculiar,
and is stained with grease and dirt,
that it's missing half its buttons,
and has got so many holes
that it might have been infested
by a regiment of moles.

Yes! I know that I've outgrown it,
that it's faded and it's torn,
I can see the sleeves are frazzled,
I'm aware the collar's worn,
but I've had that shirt forever,
and I swear that I'll be hurt
if you dare to throw that shirt out —
IT'S MY ALL-TIME FAVORITE SHIRT!

# REFLECTION

by Shel Silverstein

Each time I see the Upside-Down Man
Standing in the water,
I look at him and start to laugh,
Although I shouldn't oughtter.
For maybe in another world
Another time
Another town,
Maybe HE is right side up
And I am upside down.

# LIKE JAKE AND ME

by Mavis Jukes · pictures by Lloyd Bloom

The rain had stopped. The sun was setting. There were clouds in the sky the color of smoke. Alex was watching his stepfather, Jake, split wood at the edge of the cypress grove. Somewhere a toad was grunting.

"Jake!" called Alex.

Jake swung the axe, and wood flew into the air.

"Jake!" Alex called again. "Need me?" Alex had a loose tooth in front. He moved it in and out with his tongue.

Jake rested the axe head in the grass and leaned on the handle. "What?" he said. He took off his Stetson hat and wiped his forehead on his jacket sleeve.

Alex cupped his hands around his mouth. "Do . . . you . . . need . . . me . . . to . . . help?" he hollered. Then he tripped over a pumpkin, fell on it, and broke it. A toad flopped away.

Jake adjusted the raven feather behind his hatband. "Better stay there!" he called. He put his hat back on. With powerful arms, he sunk the axe blade into a log. It fell in half.

"Wow," thought Alex. "I'll never be able to do that."

Alex's mother was standing close by, under the pear tree. She was wearing fuzzy woolen leg warmers, a huge knitted coat with pictures of reindeer on the back, and a red scarf with the name *Virginia* on it. "I need you," she said.

Alex stood up, dumped the pumpkin over the fence for the sheep, and went to Virginia.

"I dropped two quarters and a dime in the grass. If I bend down, I may never be able to get up again," she said. Virginia was enormous. She was pregnant with twins, and her belly blocked her view to the ground. "I can't even see where they fell."

"Here!" said Alex. He gave her two quarters. Then he found the dime. He tied her shoe while he was down there.

"Thanks," said Virginia. "I also need you for some advice." She pointed up. "Think it's ready?"

One of the branches of the pear tree had a glass bottle over the end of it. Inside were some twigs and leaves *and* two pears. In the spring, Virginia had pushed the bottle onto the branch, over the blossoms. During the summer, the pears had grown and sweetened inside the bottle. Now they were fat and crowding each other.

The plan was that when the pears were ripe, Virginia would pull the bottle from the tree, leaving the fruit inside. Then she'd fill the bottle with pear nectar and trick her sister, Caroline. Caroline would never guess how Virginia got the pears into the bottle!

"Shall we pick it?" asked Virginia.

"Up to you!" said Alex.

Months ago, Virginia had told him that the pears, and the babies, would be ready in the fall. Alex looked away at the hills. They were dusky gray. There were smudges of yellow poplars on the land. Autumn was here.

Alex fiddled with his tooth. "Mom," he asked, "do you think the twins are brothers or sisters?"

"Maybe both," said Virginia.

"If there's a boy, do you think he'll be like Jake or like me?"

"Maybe like Jake *and* you," said Virginia.

"Like Jake *and* me?" Alex wondered how that could be possible.

"Right," said Virginia.

"Well, anyway," said Alex, "would you like to see something I can do?"

"Of course," she said.

Alex straightened. Gracefully he lifted his arms and rose up on his toes. He looked like a bird about to take off. Then he lowered his

arms and crouched. Suddenly he sprang up. He spun once around in midair and landed lightly.

Virginia clapped. "Great!"

Alex did it again, faster. Then again, and again. He whirled and danced around the tree for Virginia. He spun until he was pooped. Jake had put down the axe and was watching.

"Ballet class!" gasped Alex. "Dad signed me up for lessons, remember?"

"Of course I remember," said Virginia. "Go show Jake!"

"No," panted Alex. "Jake isn't the ballet type."

"He might like it," said Virginia. "Go see!"

"Maybe another time," said Alex. He raced across the field to where Jake was loading his arms with logs. "Jake, I'll carry the axe."

"Carry the axe?" Jake shook his head. "I just sharpened that axe."

Alex moved his tooth with his tongue and squinted up at Jake. "I'm careful," he said.

Jake looked over at the sheep nosing the pumpkin. "Maybe another time," he told Alex.

Alex walked beside him as they headed toward the house. The air was so cold Jake was breathing steam. The logs were stacked to his chin.

Virginia stood under the pear tree, watching the sunset. Alex ran past her to open the door.

Jake thundered up the stairs and onto the porch. His boots were covered with moss and dirt. Alex stood in the doorway.

"Watch it!" said Jake. He shoved the door open farther with his shoulder, and Alex backed up against the wall. Jake moved sideways through the door.

"Here, I'll help you stack the wood!" said Alex.

"Watch it!" Jake came down on one knee and set the wood by the side of the woodstove. Then he said kindly, "You've really got to watch it, Alex. I can't see where I'm going with so big a load."

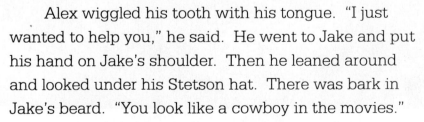

Alex wiggled his tooth with his tongue. "I just wanted to help you," he said. He went to Jake and put his hand on Jake's shoulder. Then he leaned around and looked under his Stetson hat. There was bark in Jake's beard. "You look like a cowboy in the movies."

255

"I have news for you," said Jake. "I *am* a cowboy. A real one." He unsnapped his jacket. On his belt buckle was a silver longhorn steer. "Or was one." He looked over at Alex.

Alex shoved his tooth forward with his tongue.

"Why don't you just pull out that tooth?" Jake asked him.

"Too chicken," said Alex. He closed his mouth.

"Well, everybody's chicken of something," said Jake. He opened his jacket pocket and took out a wooden match. He chewed on the end of it and looked out the windows behind the stove. He could see Virginia, still standing beneath the tree. Her hands were folded under her belly.

Jake balled up newspaper and broke some sticks. He had giant hands. He filled the woodstove with the wadded paper and the sticks and pushed in a couple of logs.

"Can I light the fire?" Alex asked.

"Maybe another time," said Jake. He struck the match on his rodeo belt buckle. He lit the paper and threw the match into the fire.

Just then Alex noticed that there was a wolf spider on the back of Jake's neck. There were fuzzy babies holding on to her body. "Did you know wolf spiders carry their babies around?" said Alex.

"Says who?" asked Jake.

"My dad," said Alex. He moved his tooth out as far as it would go. "He's an entomologist, remember?"

"I remember," said Jake.

"Dad says they only bite you if you bother them, or if you're squashing them," said Alex. "But still, I never mess with wolf spiders." He pulled his tooth back in with his tongue.

"Is that what he says, huh," said Jake. He jammed another log into the stove, then looked out again at Virginia. She was gazing at the landscape. The hills were fading. The farms were fading. The cypress trees were turning black.

"I think she's pretty," said Alex, looking at the spider.

"I do, too," said Jake, looking at Virginia.

"It's a nice design on her back," said Alex, examining the spider.

"Yep!" said Jake. He admired the reindeer coat, which he'd loaned to Virginia.

256

257

"Her belly sure is big!" said Alex.

"It has to be big, to carry the babies," said Jake.

"She's got an awful lot of babies there," said Alex.

Jake laughed. Virginia was shaped something like a pear.

"And boy! Are her legs woolly!" said Alex.

Jake looked at Virginia's leg warmers. "Itchy," said Jake. He rubbed his neck. The spider crawled over his collar.

"She's in your coat!" said Alex. He backed away a step.

"We can share it," said Jake. He liked to see Virginia bundled up. "It's big enough for both of us. She's got to stay warm." Jake stood up.

"You sure are brave," said Alex. "I like wolf spiders, but I wouldn't have let that one into my coat. That's the biggest, hairiest wolf spider I've ever seen."

Jake froze. "Wolf spider! Where?"

"In your coat getting warm," said Alex.

Jake stared at Alex. "What wolf spider?"

"The one we were talking about, with the babies!" said Alex. "And the furry legs."

"Wolf spider!" Jake moaned. "I thought we were talking about Virginia!" He was holding his shoulders up around his ears.

"You never told me you were scared of spiders," said Alex.

"You never asked me," said Jake in a high voice. "Help!"

"How?" asked Alex.

"Get my jacket off!"

Alex took hold of Jake's jacket sleeve as Jake eased his arm out. Cautiously, Alex took the jacket from Jake's shoulders. Alex looked in the coat.

"No spider, Jake," said Alex. "I think she went into your shirt."

"My shirt?" asked Jake. "You think?"

"Maybe," said Alex.

Jake gasped. "Inside? I hope not!"

"Feel anything furry crawling on you?" asked Alex.

"Anything *furry* crawling on me?" Jake shuddered. "No!"

"Try to get your shirt off without squashing her," said Alex. "Remember, we don't want to hurt her. She's a mama."

"With babies," added Jake. *"Eek!"*

"And," said Alex, "she'll bite!"

"Bite? Yes, I know!" said Jake. "Come out on the porch and help me! I don't want her to get loose in the house!"

Jake walked stiffly to the door. Alex opened it. They walked out onto the porch. The sky was thick gray and salmon colored, with blue windows through the clouds.

"Feel anything?" asked Alex.

"Something . . ." said Jake. He unsnapped the snaps on his sleeves, then the ones down the front. He opened his shirt. On his chest was a tattoo of an eagle that was either taking off or landing. He let the shirt drop to the floor.

"No spider, back or front," reported Alex.

They shook out the shirt.

"Maybe your jeans," said Alex. "Maybe she got into your jeans!"

"Not my *jeans!*" said Jake. He quickly undid his rodeo belt.

"Your boots!" said Alex. "First you have to take off your boots!"

"Right!" said Jake. He sat down on the boards. Each boot had a yellow rose and the name *Jake* stitched on the side. "Could you help?" he asked.

"Okay," said Alex. He grappled with one boot and got it off. He checked it. He pulled off and checked the sock. No spider. He tugged on the other boot.

"You've got to pull harder," said Jake, as Alex pulled and struggled. "Harder!"

The boot came off and smacked Alex in the mouth. "Ouch!" Alex put his tongue in the gap. "Knocked my tooth out!" He looked in the boot. "It's in the boot!"

"Yikes!" said Jake.

"Not the spider," said Alex. "My tooth." He rolled it out of the boot and into his hand to examine it.

"Dang," said Jake. "Then hurry up." Alex dropped the tooth back into the boot. Jake climbed out of his jeans and looked down each leg. He hopped on one foot to get the other sock off.

"She won't be in your sock," said Alex. "But maybe — "

"Don't tell me," said Jake. "Not my shorts!"

Alex stared at Jake's shorts. There were pictures of mallard ducks on them. "Your shorts," said Alex.

261

"I'm afraid to look," said Jake. He thought he felt something creeping just below his belly button.

"Someone's coming!" said Alex. "Quick! Give me your hat! I'll hold it up and you can stand behind it."

"Help!" said Jake in a small voice. He gave Alex the hat and quickly stepped out of his shorts. He brushed himself off in the front.

"Okay in the back," said Alex, peering over the brim of the hat.

Jake turned his shorts inside out, then right side in again. No spider. When he bent over to put them on, he backed into his hat, and the raven feather poked him. Jake howled and jumped up and spun around in midair.

"I didn't know you could do ballet!" said Alex. "You dance like me!"

"I thought I felt the spider!" said Jake. He put on his shorts.

"What on *earth* are you doing?" huffed Virginia. She was standing at the top of the stairs, holding the bottle with the pears inside.

"We're hunting for a spider," said Jake.

"Well!" said Virginia. "I like your hunting outfit. But aren't those *duck*-hunting shorts, and aren't you cold?"

"We're not hunting spiders," explained Jake. "We're hunting *for* a spider."

"A big and hairy one that *bites!*" added Alex.

"A wolf spider!" said Jake, shivering. He had goose bumps.

"Really!" said Virginia. She set the bottle down beside Jake's boot. "Aha!" she cried, spying Alex's tooth inside. "Here's one of the spider's teeth!"

Alex grinned at his mother. He put his tongue where his tooth wasn't.

Jake took his hat from Alex and put it on.

"Hey!" said Virginia.

"What?" said Jake.

"The spider!" she said. "It's on your hat!"

"Help!" said Jake. "Somebody help me!"

Alex sprang up into the air and snatched the hat from Jake's head.

"Look!" said Alex.

"Holy smoke!" said Jake.

There, hiding behind the black feather, was the spider.

Alex tapped the hat brim. The spider dropped to the floor. Then off she swaggered with her fuzzy babies, across the porch and into a crack.

Jake went over to Alex. He knelt down. "Thanks, Alex," said Jake. It was the closest Alex had ever been to the eagle. Jake pressed Alex against its wings. "May I have this dance?" Jake asked.

Ravens were lifting from the blackening fields and calling. The last light had settled in the clouds like pink dust.

Jake stood up holding Alex, and together they looked at Virginia. She was rubbing her belly. "Something is happening here," she told them. "It feels like the twins are beginning to dance."

"Like Jake and me," said Alex. And Jake whirled around the porch with Alex in his arms.

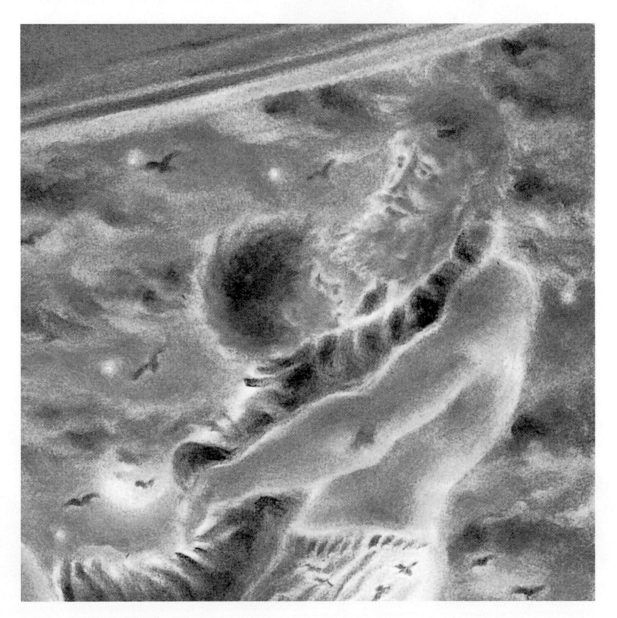

# Meet the Author
# Mavis Jukes

**M**avis Jukes's experiences with one of her own stepsons inspired her to write *Like Jake and Me.* As in the story, a shared "act of courage" brought Jukes and her stepson closer. She dared Cannon, her nine-year-old stepson, to tap-dance in front of a theater full of people. He dared her to join him, and together they danced "like two dopes" across the stage. "I'll never forget it, ever," says Jukes, "because it was the first time Cannon had ever held my hand."

Mavis Jukes also has two daughters. The older one sparked Jukes's switch from a career in law to writing. "One day I wrote a story for her," Jukes remembers. "When I saw what I had written, I realized I was a writer."

Jukes thinks that there are lots of people who simply don't realize that they are writers. And she wants to encourage them: "If you love to tell stories, if you love to hear stories, if you love words and how people speak them, you may be a writer. If you notice things — bees changing places on flowers, a plastic bag blowing down the street in the dark . . . you may be a writer. If you love movies and music, you may be a writer."

Jukes has written many award-winning books for young readers. *Like Jake and Me* was a 1985 Newbery Honor book. You might also enjoy *Blackberries in the Dark* and *No One Is Going to Nashville.*

# Meet the Illustrator Lloyd Bloom

**W**hen Lloyd Bloom illustrates a book, he responds to it with a special style that brings out the best in the author's story. Sometimes he creates black-and-white drawings, other times colorful paintings. For *Like Jake and Me,* Bloom went even further, discovering a new way of painting with pastels that brings Mavis Jukes's story vividly to life.

Bloom has been working at his art ever since he was a teenager in New York City. He has studied many kinds of art, including painting, drawing, and sculpture. In addition to *Like Jake and Me,* Bloom has illustrated many other books for young people. Some of them include *Grey Cloud,* by Charlotte Towner Graeber; *Arthur, For the Very First Time,* by Patricia MacLachlan; and *A Man Named Thoreau,* by Robert Burleigh.

# SPIN OUT YOUR IDEAS

## Illustrate a Scene

### Picture This

Mavis Jukes's colorful descriptions help readers visualize the story. When you read *Like Jake and Me,* what pictures came to *your* mind? Draw something in the story that isn't already illustrated, or draw another view of something that is. Use the story's descriptions as your guide.

## Hold a Discussion

### To Each His Own

Jake and Alex have different reactions to the wolf spider. Discuss the way each of them respond. Then talk about things that scare other people but don't scare you.

## What's in a Title?

Think about the title of the selection *Like Jake and Me.* Why do you think Mavis Jukes gave her story that name? Write a paragraph telling what the title means to you.

I AM NOT SCARED OF THESE!

## Live and Learn

Think about *Like Jake and Me* and *In the Year of the Boar and Jackie Robinson.* Shirley and Alex each go through learning experiences. Have a discussion about what each of these main characters learns. How are Shirley and Alex alike and how do they differ?

# Try to See It . . . . . . . .

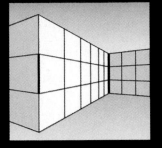

**The Long and Short of It**  Are the dark lines in this picture the same length? Perspective makes your brain say *no*, but what does your ruler say?

**Parallel Lines?**  The short hash marks on these long lines make them appear to veer away from each other. But do they really? Lift the bottom edge of your book and look across the picture from the lower left corner — and get a straight answer!

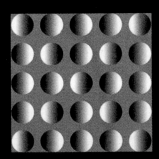

**Shading and Shape**  The sun provides constant "overhead lighting," which your brain uses to help define shapes. Here, light is hitting the circles from different sides, so your brain can't really "decide" on their shape. If you turn the picture 90 degrees to the left or right, however, the light comes from "above." Then you can see an X of either concave (inward) or convex (outward) circles.

**Which Is It?**  This vase was made for England's Queen Elizabeth II and Prince Philip. When you look at it, what do you see? A vase with an irregular shape — or the profiles of Elizabeth (right) and Philip (left)? Your brain can recognize both, but not at the same time. Either the vase or the profiles could be the background — or the foreground — so they jump back and forth before your eyes.

# ... If You Can!

Artists and architects use light, color, shape — and the way your brain works — to fool and delight your eyes!

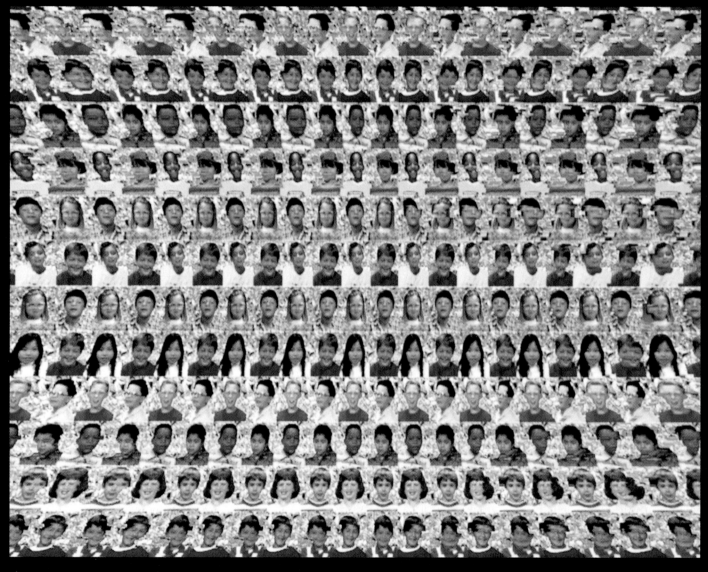

**Patience Makes Perfect** Explore the exciting world of three-dimensional imaging. When you stare "through" the repeating patterns, a new, 3-D image gradually appears. Try it — but don't look "at" the new image or it'll disappear!

▲
**An Artistic Breakthrough** The artist of this mural on a water tank in Sacramento, California, used a nearly photographic painting technique called *trompe l'oeil* ("fool the eye") to make this superhero appear to smash through the wall.

**Which Way Is Up?** Dutch graphic artist M. C. Escher called this visual riddle "Relativity." The whole picture is confusing, but look at each staircase separately and it makes perfect sense.

**Building Art** It reflects the street, neighboring buildings, and the sky. The architect designed this skyscraper in downtown Winnipeg, Manitoba, to both stand out and disappear in its environment.

The goal of advertisers is to make you see things their way. The "Bug Squad," a monthly feature in *Zillions* magazine, helps you see through the words – and numbers – advertisers use to pitch their clients' products.

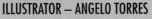
ILLUSTRATOR — ANGELO TORRES

# Me, Mop, and the Moondance Kid

## BY WALTER DEAN MYERS

Mop, T.J., and T.J.'s brother, Moondance, once lived together at the Dominican Academy, a home for orphans. T.J. and Moondance have been adopted, but Mop — and Taffy, the Academy llama — face an uncertain future if the Academy closes. Meanwhile, the Elks, the kids' baseball team, is trying hard to get into the play-offs. The team has lots of boosters: Marla, the coach; Sister Carmelita of the Academy; and Peaches, a neighborhood character. But the team also has its doubters. Mr. Treaster, a rival coach, keeps laughing at the Elks. T.J. and Moondance's adoptive father, once a professional ballplayer, is growing impatient. And T.J. is beginning to doubt himself.

Saturday was the day of the Pumas' game and I was really excited. Dad asked three times when the game was going to start. I was in a good mood, but it didn't last too long. When me and Moondance got to the Academy to pick up Mop, we got some bad news about Taffy. The zoo didn't want her after all.

"What will they do with her?" Moondance asked.

Sister Carmelita shrugged. "Maybe we can find a farm that will take her," she said. "There are a lot of llama farms out west."

"Let's get to the game," Mop said. "We'll talk about Taffy later."

We had to play the Pumas, and then we had to play the Hawks. If we beat the Pumas, then we would have second place and be in the play-offs against the first-place team which we knew already was going to be the Eagles. If we lost to the Pumas, we could still get into the play-offs by beating the Hawks.

"We want to beat the Pumas," Marla said when we got to the field. "If we do, then we can relax a little bit for the last game before the play-offs."

"We're not going to win the play-offs against no Eagles," Evans said. "They too good."

"We have a chance in a short series," Marla said. "We just have to win two games out of the three."

"How we gonna win two games when we ain't never won once against them?" Evans said.

"We're better than we were when we first played them," Marla said. "And we'll prove it."

Mike pitched for us and the Pumas scored five runs in the first inning. I wasn't playing. Marla had Lo Vinh playing third base instead of me.

"Why aren't you playing third base?" Dad had shown up shortly after the game started. "That kid they have out there now doesn't look that good."

"I don't know," I said. "Maybe Marla just wants to let him play for a while."

Dad's jaw tightened a little. And then he went up into the stands to watch the game.

By the third inning the score was 15 to 3 and I knew we were going to lose. Dad was right about Lo Vinh not being too good at third base. But then he hurt his hand and Marla brought in Jennifer! You ever see Jennifer play? If the ball goes two feet away from her, she won't even go for it.

Brian got mad and threw his glove down and Marla told him if he did that again, he would come out of the game.

"Hey, Marla, you got a great squad there!" Joe Treaster had shown up and was leaning against the fence. "I hope they make the play-offs!"

"So do I," Marla said.

A guy came down to the field and said he thought Marla should put Moondance on third base and put Jennifer in the outfield.

"You go back into the stands and I will run this team!" Marla said in this real loud voice.

"Tell him, baby!" Mr. Treaster yelled again.

In the fifth inning we scored two runs and everybody got happy again. Marla switched Brian from short to pitcher and put Mike on short-stop. We were still way behind though.

276

277

In the top of the sixth Brian struck out the first Puma and Mop made a diving catch of a pop foul for the second out. The next two batters bunted balls down the third base line toward Jennifer. She didn't even try to run in for them. Brian got so mad he threw his glove at her. That's when Marla took him out of the game.

Brian's father was yelling at Marla. Mr. Treaster was yelling at her and laughing. I looked around to see what my Dad was doing and I saw him talking to Sister Carmelita.

"Hey! T.J.! Wake up!"

I turned and saw that Marla was pointing at me. I got my glove and went over to her.

She switched Mike back to pitcher, brought Joey DeLea in to play shortstop and put me in right field.

"Come on, guys," Marla said. "Let's prove we can stop them when we have to."

Mike loaded the bases by walking the next batter. Then their best hitter got up. He swung at the first pitch.

I could hear the crack of the bat and saw the ball coming right out to me. It looked like it was growing bigger as it came.

I went running in for it.  I knew I was going to catch it.  It came down and down.  I was banging my glove with my fist.  I was all ready to catch it.

It was a little higher than I thought.

I went back two steps and reached up as far as I could.  The ball flew just over my glove.  It bounced over the fence for an automatic double.

Everybody in the infield was throwing their gloves down and looking at me.  Everybody.

Even from where I was standing, way in the outfield, all by myself, I could see Dad shaking his head.  I knew what he was thinking.  He was wondering how come he had such a lousy kid playing ball.

They scored one more run and then we got up.  When I went in, I saw Marla talking to everybody.  Then when I got to the bench they all said things like "Nice try" and "You almost had it."  But nobody looked at me and I knew that Marla had told them to say that.

We didn't score that inning, but neither did the Pumas during the top of the seventh.

I got up in the last of the seventh.  There were two outs and I missed the first two pitches.  Then I bunted at the next ball and hit it but it went foul.  Then the umpire called me out because of a rule about a foul bunt on the third strike being an out.

The Pumas won, 18 to 5.

After the game I didn't even want to go near Dad.  He came over to where me and Jennifer were packing up the bases in the old blue duffel bag that we carried our stuff in and went up to Marla.

"Tough loss," he said.

"They're all tough losses, Mr. Williams," Marla said.

"Titi said that you might actually make the play-offs."  Dad shifted his weight from one foot to the other.  "I can't see how you're going to win."

I pushed home plate as hard as I could down to the bottom of the bag.

"I don't know who this Titi is," Marla said.  "But he might have also told you that we scored some runs against this team.  If we had another pitcher besides Brian, if Moondance could throw the ball over the plate, for example, we would have a chance of at least being respectable."

282

"Why don't you let Titi help?" Dad said. "She used to be the best pitcher in our league."

"In the first place, I don't know this Titi," Marla said. "And I think it's a little late with the play-offs starting next week."

"You don't know Sister Carmelita?" Dad asked.

"Sister Carmelita?"

"Yeah, way back before she was a nun she used to play Little League ball right here in Lincoln Park," Dad said. "We used to call her Titi then. And she could *pitch*!"

Okay, so Sister Carmelita used to be a pitcher. But do you know who really helped Moondance turn out to be a good pitcher? Peaches! Okay, Peaches *and* Sister Carmelita.

Marla talked to Sister Carmelita and asked if she could help Moondance. Sister Carmelita said that she didn't know, but she would try. So we all went out to the playground the next day and Dad put the Sunday comics on the ground for the plate. Moondance started pitching to Mop.

Zip! Zip! Zip!

He could throw that ball over the plate so fast it wasn't even funny.

Zip! Zip! Zip!

283

Marla shook her head.

"Let's see how you hold the ball, Moondance." Sister Carmelita looked at how Moondance held the ball in his hand.

"Like this," Moondance said, holding the ball up.

Sister Carmelita held his hand still and moved the ball a little. "Try it that way," she said. "Don't let it touch your palm. It's a little trickier, but I think you can do it."

The first ball that Moondance threw went right over Mop's head.

"Follow through!" Sister Carmelita called out. "Bring your arm all the way down."

Zip! Whack!

That's the way the ball went. It went even faster than it did the first time he was throwing.

Zip! Whack!

The next ball went over Mop's head, but after that the ball was going right into the glove.

Zip! Whack!

Zip! Whack!

"T.J., stand at the plate." Marla handed me a bat.

No way I wanted to stand there with the bat. I looked at Marla to see if she really meant for me to stand there, but she had already gone over to sit on one of the benches. Dad was leaning against the backstop and Sister Carmelita was standing near Moondance out at the mound. It was as if they were watching a show or something.

I looked at Moondance and he looked at me. He had his tongue out and was wiping off his pitching hand. Mop got down on her knees and put one hand behind her back.

"Throw it past him, Moondance!" she yelled. "He can't hit!"

"Don't swing, T.J.," Marla called out. "I just want to see his control."

Zip!

The ball went outside and against the backstop. Dad looked at Moondance and one eyebrow went up. Mop got the ball and threw it back to Moondance. Sister Carmelita was talking to him, but I couldn't hear what she was saying.

You know how I felt? A little nervous. Even though I didn't have to swing at the ball, you get a little nervous when Moondance throws it with all of his might.

Zip!

The ball went outside and past Mop's glove again.

"Give him a target, Mop!"

"I am giving him a target!" Mop yelled back as she picked the ball up again.

"C'mon, Son." Dad made a fist and held it up toward Moondance. "Bring it high and tight."

I didn't know what that meant, but I saw the next ball go flying outside again.

"Stand on the other side, T.J."

That's what Marla said.

"No!" That's what I said. Moondance was throwing the balls just where she wanted me to stand.

"You're not scared of the ball, are you?" Dad asked.

"No," I said.

I went to the other side. I wasn't scared of the ball. I mean, if the ball and me were in a dark room together, I wouldn't be nervous or anything. I was afraid of being *hit* by the ball.

Moondance wound up and threw the ball. I dropped the bat and got ready to duck in case it came toward me, but it didn't. It went on the other side.

"Moondance, are you afraid of hitting him?" Marla got off the bench and started toward us.

"I don't want to hit anybody," Moondance said.

"Don't worry about it, just throw the ball to Hop," Dad said.

"That's Mop, *M-O-P*." Mop gave Dad a look.

"If you just aim for Mop's glove, you won't be that close to him," Marla said. "You can almost do it with your eyes closed."

I got away from the plate. He wasn't throwing the ball at me with his eyes closed.

"Just keep your eye on the glove," Sister Carmelita said. "Take your time."

Moondance looked at Mop's glove and kept his eyes right on it. He wound up and threw the ball again.

Zip!

Fast as anything, but outside. I think they were right. He didn't want to hit me.

Then Dad caught and Mop got up to bat. Same thing. Moondance didn't want to throw the ball near anybody.

Dad said he would talk to him and I saw Moondance look a little sad. Sometimes Dad says things that sound good, or at least okay, but deep down you know they're not. He said he would talk to Moondance, that everything would be okay. But you could tell by the way he said it that he wasn't happy with the way Moondance pitched. I could tell it and Moondance could tell it too.

It's bad when you mess up and people aren't happy with you. Like when I missed the fly ball and everybody on the team threw their gloves down. But I think it's even worse when you do something good, like Moondance did, and somebody isn't happy with you because you didn't do it good enough. Especially when that somebody is your dad.

Still, Sister Carmelita had helped Moondance a little, and we didn't even know that Peaches was going to help too.

When we got home, Dad got out all these pictures of him playing baseball. He looked great. I imagined myself doing some of the things he did.

WILLIAMS'S HOMER SPURS ASU WIN!

"That's when we won the national championship," Dad said. "We made every paper in the state of Arizona every day that week!"

"That's where I first met him," Mom said. "All he ever talked about then was playing baseball. All he ever did was play baseball too. I think he married me because I could keep score."

Then he showed us the pictures of himself when he played for Kansas City.

"It must be hard to be a great baseball player," I said.

"Sometimes," Dad said. "It's even harder not to be a great ballplayer."

291

# WALTER DEAN MYERS
## AUTHOR

**W**alter Dean Myers likes to write for young people. He hopes they will see themselves in his stories. Myers says, "When kids find . . . a good character who makes them say look, here I am in this book, this guy feels the same way I do — it's reassuring."

Myers used some of his own experiences in writing *Me, Mop, and the Moondance Kid.* Like T.J., he was raised by adoptive parents. At the age of three, he went to live with the Dean family in the Harlem section of New York City. There he found a close community that helped him believe in himself. Many of Myers's more than thirty books draw on those early years.

You can follow the further adventures of T.J. and his friends in *Mop, Moondance, and the Nagasaki Knights.* Read what happens when the Elks face a baseball team from Japan.

# ANTHONY WOOLRIDGE
## ILLUSTRATOR

A lifelong resident of Virginia, Anthony Woolridge has been drawing and painting since the age of six. His grandfather, a farmer who raised chickens, pigs, and goats, encouraged Woolridge's interest in nature. "I wasn't the play-around-in-the-city type," Woolridge recalls. He had something else in common with T.J., Mop, and Moondance, however. He grew up with friends of many cultures. He remembers what it was like to be part of a group of "different people finding a common goal."

# Put Your Ideas in Play!

## What Did He Mean?

At the end of the selection, Mr. Williams says, "Sometimes it's even harder not to be a great ballplayer." What do you think he means? Share your thoughts in a small group or with the class.

## I Remember . . .

When T. J. and his family return home after the game, Mr. Williams shows photographs from his days as a baseball player. If T. J. were to create a scrapbook of his own, what would he put in it? Brainstorm some ideas. Then put together a scrapbook for T. J.

## I'll Trade You!

Make a baseball card for each of your favorite characters in *Me, Mop, and the Moondance Kid.* Draw a picture of each character and write his or her name on one side of the card. Write a brief description of the character on the back of the card.

**Compare Selections**

## Great Expectations

Think about the characters in *Me, Mop, and the Moondance Kid, Like Jake and Me,* and *In the Year of the Boar and Jackie Robinson.* T. J., Alex, and Shirley all try to please someone by behaving in a certain way. Write a few sentences explaining what each character is trying to do and why. Then write about a time when you tried to live up to someone else's expectations.

# We Could Be Friends

by Myra Cohn Livingston

We could be friends
Like friends are supposed to be.
You, picking up the telephone
Calling me

to come over and play
or take a walk,
finding a place
to sit and talk,

Or just goof around
Like friends do,
Me, picking up the telephone
Calling you.

# Narcissa

## by Gwendolyn Brooks

Some of the girls are playing jacks.
Some are playing ball.
But small Narcissa is not playing
Anything at all.

Small Narcissa sits upon
A brick in her back yard
And looks at tiger lilies,
And shakes her pigtails hard.

First she is an ancient queen
In pomp and purple veil.
Soon she is a singing wind.
And, next, a nightingale.

How fine to be Narcissa,
A-changing like all that!
While sitting still, as still, as still
As anyone ever sat!

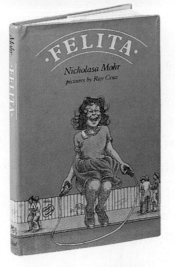

# Felita
## by Nicholasa Mohr

A wonderful thing happened this new school year. Gigi, Consuela, Paquito, and I were all going into the fourth grade, and we were put in the same class. It had never happened before. Once I was in the same class with Consuela, and last year Gigi and Paquito were together. But this — it was too good to be true! Of course knowing Gigi and I were in the same class made me the happiest.

Our teacher, Miss Lovett, was friendly and laughed easily. In early October, after we had all settled into our class and gotten used to the routine of school once more, Miss Lovett told us that this year our class was going to put on a play for Thanksgiving. The play we were going to perform was based on a poem by Henry Wadsworth Longfellow, called "The Courtship of Miles Standish." It was about the Pilgrims and how they lived when they first landed in America.

We were all so excited about the play. Miss Lovett called for volunteers to help with the sets and costumes. Paquito and I agreed to help with the sets. Consuela was going to work on makeup. Gigi had not volunteered for anything. When we asked her what she was going to do, she shrugged and didn't answer.

Miss Lovett said we could all audition for the different parts in the play. I was really interested in being Priscilla. She is the heroine. Both Captain Miles Standish and the handsome, young John Alden are in love with her. She is the most beautiful maiden in Plymouth, Massachusetts. That's where the Pilgrims used to live. I told my friends how much I would like to play that part. Everyone said I would be perfect . . . except Gigi. She said that it was a hard part to do, and maybe I wouldn't be able to play it. I really got annoyed and asked her what she meant.

"I just don't think you are right to play Priscilla. That's all," she said.

"What do you mean by right?" I asked. But Gigi only shrugged and didn't say another word. She was beginning to get on my nerves.

Auditions for the parts were going to start Tuesday. Lots of kids had volunteered to audition. Paquito said he would try out for the brave Captain Miles Standish. Consuela said she was too afraid to get up in front of everybody and make a fool of herself. Gigi didn't show any interest in the play and refused to even talk to us about it. Finally the day came for the girls to read for the part of Priscilla. I was so excited I could hardly wait. Miss Lovett had given us some lines to study. I had practiced real hard. She called out all the names of those who were going to read. I was surprised when I heard her call out "Georgina Mercado." I didn't even know Gigi wanted to try out for Priscilla. I looked at Gigi, but she ignored me. We began reading. It was my turn. I was very nervous and kept forgetting my lines. I had to look down at the script a whole lot. Several other girls were almost as nervous as I was. Then it was Gigi's turn. She recited the part almost by heart. She hardly looked at the script. I noticed that she was wearing one of her best dresses. She had never looked that good in school before. When she finished, every-body clapped. It was obvious that she was the best one. Miss Lovett made a fuss.

"You were just wonderful, Georgina," she said, "made for the part!" Boy, would I have liked another chance. I bet I could have done better than Gigi.

Why hadn't she told me she wanted the part? It's a free country, after all. She could read for the same part as me. I wasn't going to stop her! I was really angry at Gigi.

After school everyone was still making a fuss over her. Even Paquito had to open his stupid mouth.

"Oh, man, Gigi!" he said. "You were really good. I liked the part when John Alden asked you to marry Captain Miles Standish and you said, 'Why don't you speak for yourself, John?' You turned your head like this." Paquito imitated Gigi and closed his eyes. "That was really neat!" Consuela and the others laughed and agreed.

I decided I wasn't walking home with them.

"I have to meet my brothers down by the next street," I said. "I'm splitting. See you." They hardly noticed. Only Consuela said goodbye. The rest just kept on hanging all over Gigi. Big deal, I thought.

Of course walking by myself and watching out for the tough kids was not something I looked forward to. Just last Friday Hilda Gonzales had gotten beat up and had her entire allowance stolen. And at the beginning of the term Paquito had been walking home by himself and gotten mugged. A bunch of big bullies had taken his new schoolbag complete with pencil and pen case, then left him with a swollen lip. No, sir, none of us ever walked home from school alone if we could help it. We knew it wasn't a safe thing to do. Those mean kids never bothered us as long as we stuck together. Carefully I looked around to make sure none of the bullies were in sight. Then I put some speed under my feet, took my chances, and headed for home.

Just before all the casting was completed, Miss Lovett offered me a part as one of the Pilgrim women. All I had to do was stand in the background like a zombie. It wasn't even a speaking part.

"I don't get to say one word," I protested.

"Felicidad Maldonado, you are designing the stage sets and you're assistant stage manager. I think that's quite a bit. Besides, all the speaking parts are taken."

"I'm not interested, thank you," I answered.

"You know" — Miss Lovett shook her head — "you can't be the best in everything."

I turned and left. I didn't need to play any part at all. Who cared?

Gigi came over to me the next day with a great big smile all over her face. I just turned away and made believe she wasn't there.

"Felita, are you taking the part of the Pilgrim woman?" she asked me in her sweetest voice, just like nothing had happened.

"No," I said, still not looking at her. If she thought I was going to fall all over her like those dummies, she was wasting her time.

302

"Oh," was all she said, and walked away. Good, I thought. I don't need her one bit!

At home Mami noticed something was wrong.

"Felita, what's the matter? You aren't going out at all. And I haven't seen Gigi for quite a while. In fact I haven't seen any of your friends."

"Nothing is the matter, Mami. I just got lots of things to do."

"You're not upset because we couldn't give you a birthday party this year, are you?" Mami asked. "You know how hard the money situation has been for us."

My birthday had been at the beginning of November. We had celebrated with a small cake after dinner, but there had been no party.

"No. It's not that," I said and meant it. Even though I had been a little disappointed, I also knew Mami and Papi had done the best they could.

"We'll make it up to you next year, Felita, you'll see."

"I don't care, Mami. It's not important now."

"You didn't go having a fight with Gigi or something? Did you?"

"Now why would I have a fight with anybody!"

"Don't raise your voice, miss," Mami said. "Sorry I asked. But you just calm down."

The play was going to be performed on the day before Thanksgiving. I made the drawings for most of the scenery. I made a barn, a church, trees and grass, cows, and a horse. I helped the others make a real scarecrow. We used a broom and old clothes. Paquito didn't get the part of Captain Miles Standish, but he made a wonderful fence out of cardboard. It looked just like a real wooden fence. Consuela brought in her mother's old leftover makeup. She did a good job of making up everybody.

By the time we set up the stage, everything looked beautiful. Gigi had tried to talk to me a few times. But I just couldn't be nice back to her. She acted like nothing had happened, like I was supposed to forget she hadn't told me she was going to read for the part! I wasn't going to forget that just because she was now Miss Popularity. She could go and stay with all her newfound friends for all I cared!

The morning of the play, at breakfast, everybody noticed how excited I was.

"Felita," Papi exclaimed, "stop jumping around like a monkey and eat your breakfast."

"She's all excited about the school play today," Mami said.

"That's right. Are you playing a part in the play?" Papi asked.

"No," I replied.

"But she's done most of the sets. Drawing and designing. Isn't that right, Felita?"

"Mami, it was no big deal."

"That's nice," said Papi. "Tell us about it."

"What kind of sets did you do?" Johnny asked.

"I don't know. Look, I don't want to talk about it."

"Boy, are you touchy today," Tito said with a laugh.

"Leave me alone!" I snapped.

"Okay." Mami stood up. "Enough. Felita, are you finished?" I nodded. "Good. Go to school. When you come back, bring home a better mood. Whatever is bothering you, no need to take it out on us." Quickly I left the table.

"Rosa," I heard Papi say, "sometimes you are too hard on her."

"And sometimes you spoil her, Alberto!" Mami snapped. "I'm not raising fresh kids."

I was glad to get out of there. Who needs them, I thought.

The play was a tremendous hit. Everybody looked wonderful and played their parts really well. The stage was brilliant with the color I had used on my drawings. The background of the countryside, the barn, and just about everything stood out clearly. Ernesto Bratter, the stage manager, said I was a good assistant. I was glad to hear that, because a couple of times I'd had to control my temper on account of his ordering me around. But it had all worked out great.

No doubt about it. Gigi was perfect as Priscilla. Even though the kids clapped and cheered for the entire cast, Gigi got more applause than anybody else. She just kept on taking a whole lot of bows.

Afterward Miss Lovett had a party for our class. We had lots of treats. There was even a record player and we all danced. We had a really good time.

Of course Priscilla, alias Gigi, was the big star. She just couldn't get enough attention. But not from me, that was for sure. After the party Gigi spoke to me.

"Your sets were really great. Everybody said the stage looked wonderful."

"Thanks." I looked away.

"Felita, are you mad at me?"

"Why should I be mad at you?"

"Well, I did get the leading part, but . . ."

"Big deal," I said. "I really don't care."

"You don't? But . . . I . . ."

"Look," I said, interrupting her, "I gotta go. I promised my mother I'd get home early. We have to go someplace."

I rushed all the way home. I didn't know why, but I was still furious at Gigi. What was worse was that I was unhappy about having those feelings. Gigi and I had been real close for as far back as I could remember. Not being able to share things with her really bothered me.

We had a great Thanksgiving. The dinner was just delicious. Abuelita brought her flan. Tío Jorge brought lots of ice cream. He always brings us kids a treat when he visits. Sometimes he even brings each one of us a small gift — a nature book or crayons for me and puzzles or sports magazines for my brothers. He's really very nice to us. One thing about him is that he's sort of quiet and doesn't talk much. Papi says that Tío Jorge has been like that as far back as he can remember.

Abuelita asked me if I wanted to go home with her that evening. Boy, was I happy to get away from Mami. I just couldn't face another day of her asking me questions about Gigi, my friends, and my whole life. It was getting to be too much!

It felt good to be with Abuelita in her apartment. Abuelita never questioned me about anything really personal unless I wanted to talk about it. She just waited, and when she sensed that I was worried or something, then she would ask me. Not like Mami. I love Mami, but she's always trying to find out every little thing that happens to me. With my abuelita sometimes we just sit and stay quiet, not talk at all. That was nice too. We fixed the daybed for me. And then Tío Jorge, Abuelita, and I had more flan as usual.

"Would you like to go to the park with me this Sunday?" Tío Jorge asked me.

"Yes."

"We can go to the zoo and later we can visit the ducks and swans by the lake."

"Great!" I said.

Whenever Tío Jorge took me to the zoo, he would tell me stories about how he, Abuelita, and their brothers and sisters had lived and worked as youngsters taking care of farm animals. These were the only times I ever heard him talk a whole lot.

"It's not just playing, you know," he would say. "Taking care of animals is hard work. Back on our farm in Puerto Rico we worked hard, but we had fun too. Every one of us children had our very own favorite pets. I had a pet goat by the name of Pepe. He used to follow me everywhere." No matter how many times he told me the same stories, I always enjoyed hearing them again.

"Well." Tío Jorge got up. "It's a date then on Sunday, yes?"

"Yes, thank you, Tío Jorge."

"Good night," he said and went off to bed.

Abuelita and I sat quietly for a while, then Abuelita spoke.

"You are getting to be a big girl now, Felita. You just turned nine years old. My goodness! But I still hope you will come to bed with your abuelita for a little while, eh?"

I got into bed and snuggled close to Abuelita. I loved her the best, more than anybody. I hadn't been to stay with her since the summer, and

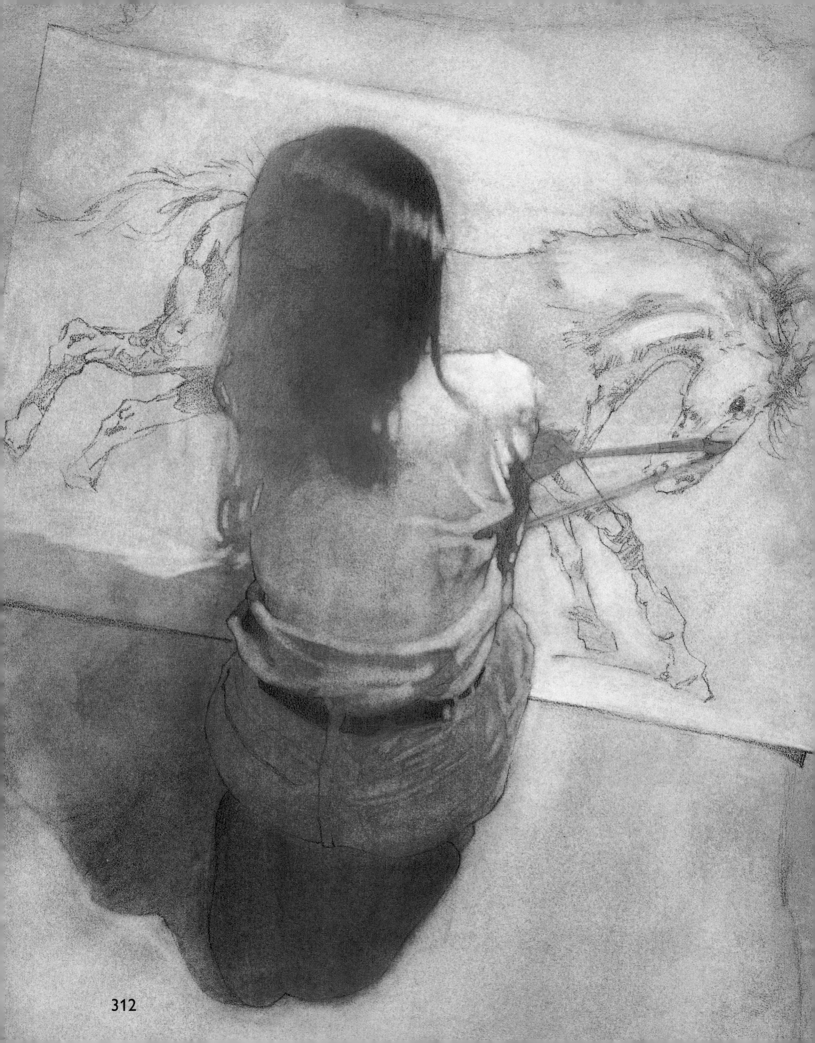

312

somehow this time things felt different. I noticed how tired Abuelita looked. She wasn't moving as fast as she used to. Also I didn't feel so little next to her anymore.

"Tell me, Felita, how have you been? It seems like a long time since we were together like this." She smiled her wonderful smile at me. Her dark, bright eyes looked deeply into mine. I felt her warmth and happiness.

"I'm okay, Abuelita."

"Tell me about your play at school. Rosa tells me you worked on the stage sets. Was the play a success?"

"It was. It was great. The stage looked beautiful. My drawings stood out really well. I never made such big drawings in my life. There was a farm in the country, a barn, and animals. I made it the way it used to be in the olden days of the Pilgrims. You know, how it was when they first came to America."

"I'm so proud of you. Tell me about the play. Did you act in it?"

"No." I paused. "I didn't want to."

"I see. Tell me a little about the story."

I told Abuelita all about it.

"Who played the parts? Any of your friends?"

"Some."

"Who?"

"Well, this boy Charlie Martinez played John Alden. Louie Collins played Captain Miles Standish. You don't know them. Mary Jackson played the part of the narrator. That's the person who tells the story. You really don't know any of them."

I was hoping she wouldn't ask, but she did.

"Who played the part of the girl both men love?"

"Oh, her? Gigi."

"Gigi Mercado, your best friend?" I nodded. "Was she good?"

"Yes, she was. Very good."

"You don't sound too happy about that."

"I don't care." I shrugged.

"But if she is your best friend, I should think you would care."

"I . . . I don't know if she is my friend anymore, Abuelita."

"Why do you say that?"

I couldn't answer. I just felt awful.

"Did she do something? Did you two argue?" I nodded. "Can I ask what happened?"

"Well, it's hard to explain. But what she did wasn't fair."

"Fair about what, Felita?"

I hadn't spoken about it before. Now with Abuelita it was easy to talk about it.

"Well, we all tried out for the different parts. Everybody knew what everybody was trying out for. But Gigi never told anybody she was going to try out for Priscilla. She kept it a great big secret. Even after I told her that I wanted to try for the part, she kept quiet about it. Do you know what she did say? She said I wasn't right for it . . . it was a hard part and all that bunch of baloney. She just wanted the part for herself, so she was mysterious about the whole thing. Like . . . it was . . . I don't know." I stopped for a moment, trying to figure this whole thing out. "After all, I am supposed to be her best friend . . . her very best friend. Why shouldn't she let me know that she wanted to be Priscilla? I wouldn't care. I let her know my plans. I didn't go sneaking around."

"Are you angry because Gigi got the part?"

It was hard for me to answer. I thought about it for a little while. "Abuelita, I don't think so. She was really good in the part."

"Were you as good when you tried out for Priscilla?"

"No." I looked at Abuelita. "I stunk." We both laughed.

"Then maybe you are not angry at Gigi at all."

"What do you mean?"

"Well, maybe you are a little bit . . . hurt?"

"Hurt?" I felt confused.

"Do you know what I think? I think you are hurt because your best friend didn't trust you. From what you tell me, you trusted her, but she didn't have faith in you. What do you think?"

"Yes." I nodded. "Abuelita, yes. I don't know why. Gigi and I always tell each other everything. Why did she act like that to me?"

"Have you asked her?"

"No."

"Why not? Aren't you two speaking to each other?"

"We're speaking. Gigi tried to be friendly a few times."

"Don't you want to stay her friend?"

"I do. Only she came over to me acting like . . . like nothing ever happened. And something did happen! What does she think? That she can go around being sneaky and I'm going to fall all over her? Just because she got the best part, she thinks she's special."

"And you think that's why she came over. Because she wants to be special?"

"I don't know."

"You should give her a chance. Perhaps Gigi acted in a strange way for a reason."

"She wasn't nice to me, Abuelita. She wasn't."

"I'm not saying she was. Or even that she was right. *Mira*, Felita, friendship is one of the best things in this whole world. It's one of the few things you can't go out and buy. It's like love. You can buy clothes, food, even luxuries, but there's no place I know of where you can buy a real friend. Do you?"

I shook my head. Abuelita smiled at me and waited. We were both silent for a long moment. I wondered if maybe I shouldn't have a talk with Gigi. After all, she had tried to talk to me first.

"Abuelita, do you think it's a good idea for me to . . . maybe talk to Gigi?"

"You know, that's a very good idea." Abuelita nodded.

"Well, she did try to talk to me a few times. Only there's just one thing. I won't know what to say to her. I mean, after what's happened and all."

"After so many years of being close, I am sure you could say 'Hello, Gigi. How are you?' That should be easy enough."

"I feel better already, Abuelita."

"Good," Abuelita said. "Now let's you and I get to sleep. Abuelita is tired."

"You don't have to tuck me in. I'll tuck you in instead." I got out of bed and folded the covers carefully over my side. Then I leaned over her and gave her a kiss. Abuelita hugged me real tight.

"My Felita has become a young lady," she whispered.

I kept thinking of what Abuelita had said, and on Monday I waited for Gigi after school. It was as if she knew I wanted to talk. She came over to me.

"Hello, Gigi," I said. "How are you?"

"Fine." Gigi smiled. "Wanna walk home together?"

"Let's take the long way so we can be by ourselves," I said.

We walked without saying anything for a couple of blocks. Finally I spoke.

"I wanted to tell you, Gigi, you were really great as Priscilla."

"Did you really like me? Oh, Felita, I'm so glad. I wanted you to like me, more than anybody else. Of course it was nothing compared to the sets you did. They were something special. Everybody liked them so much."

"You were right too," I said. "I wasn't very good for the part of Priscilla."

"Look." Gigi stopped walking and looked at me. "I'm sorry about . . . about the way I acted. Like, I didn't say anything to you or the others. But, well, I was scared you all would think I was silly or something. I mean, you wanted the part too. So, I figured, better not say nothing."

"I wouldn't have cared, Gigi. Honest."

"Felita . . . it's just that you are so good at a lot of things. Like, you draw just fantastic. You beat everybody at hopscotch and kick-the-can. You know about nature and animals, much more than the rest of us. Everything you do is always better than . . . what I do! I just wanted this part for me. I wanted to be better than you this time. For once I didn't wanna worry about you. Felita, I'm sorry."

I was shocked. I didn't know Gigi felt that way. I didn't feel better than anybody about anything I did. She looked so upset, like she was about to cry any minute. I could see she was miserable and I wanted to comfort her. I had never had this kind of feeling before in my whole life.

"Well, you didn't have to worry. 'Cause I stunk!" We both laughed with relief. "I think I was the worst one!"

"Oh, no, you weren't." Gigi laughed. "Jenny Fuentes was the most awful."

"Worse than me?"

"Much worse. Do you know what she sounded like? She sounded like this. 'Wha . . . wha . . . why don't you . . . speeek for your . . . yourself *Johnnnn*?" Gigi and I burst into laughter.

"And how about that dummy, Louie Collins? I didn't think he read better than Paquito."

"Right," Gigi agreed. "I don't know how he got through the play. He was shaking so much that I was scared the sets would fall right on his head."

It was so much fun, Gigi and I talking about the play and how we felt about everybody and everything. It was just like before, only better.

# Meet Nicholasa Mohr

Nicholasa Mohr has been putting pictures and words together since she was a child. "From the moment my mother handed me some scrap paper, a pencil, and a few crayons," she remembers, "I discovered that by making pictures and writing letters I could create my own world."

Mohr grew up as a member of a Puerto Rican family in New York City's Hispanic neighborhood, *El Barrio*. The world of *El Barrio*, however, seldom appeared in the books Mohr read while growing up. "I had never really seen myself, my brothers, or my family in those books," she recalls. Later, Mohr was inspired to re-create the world of her childhood in books she wrote herself.

Mohr worked as an artist until an editor saw her creative word-picture "graffiti" and asked her to try writing stories. Since then she has written four children's books and has illustrated two of them. Felita's story continues in the book *Going Home*.

# Meet Kevin Beilfuss

When Kevin Beilfuss (pronounced *BAIL fyoos*) was growing up, he loved sports. His favorite sport is softball — he now helps coach a girls' softball team — but football comes in a close second. When he isn't playing ball or working on his illustrations, Beilfuss plays chess. "It's a great way to take a break and exercise your mind at the same time," he says. In the future, Beilfuss hopes to add sculpture and children's book illustration to his fine-arts experience.

# Act on Your Ideas

## Between Friends

How did the misunderstanding between Felita and Gigi get started? How could it have been cleared up earlier? Discuss these questions in small groups. Then compare your solutions with those of other groups.

## Don't Call Us, We'll Call You

According to Felita and Gigi, the auditions for the Thanksgiving play were as entertaining as the play itself. Take the parts of students in Felita's class, and role-play the auditions. Don't be afraid to ham it up!

## Through Gigi's Eyes

All through the selection, Felita fumes over Gigi's playing Priscilla in the class play. How does Gigi feel about the way Felita is behaving? Write a dramatic monologue or letter in which Gigi explains her feelings to her own *abuelita*.

**Compare Selections**

## Way to Go!

In each of the selections in this theme, one or more characters overcome a problem. List the characters and the problems they solve. Who do you think does the best job solving his or her problem? Write a persuasive argument explaining your opinion.

# Living with a Hearing Impairment

## by the Westridge Young Writers Workshop

KIDS EXPLORE
the Gifts of
Children with
Special Needs

WESTRIDGE YOUNG
WRITERS WORKSHOP

WRITTEN BY KIDS!

Gena Perry at home with her two
sisters, Michaela and Brianna

**Gena (right) with her friend Christy**

## In Gena's Own Words

Would you like to get to know me better? I would like to get better acquainted with you, too! It's easy to do — just talk to me. I have noticed that sometimes people are afraid to talk to me because they know that I am hearing impaired. They are worried that I won't understand them. Don't worry, if I don't understand something you say, I will ask you about it.

It helps if you stand where I can see your face (it's hard to read your lips when all I can see is the back of your head!). Also, if you stand with the sun or a bright light behind your head, sometimes shadows get on your face and it is hard to see your mouth. You don't need to talk really slow or really loud. Especially, please don't exaggerate how you enunciate each word. All those things distort the words you are saying. Remember, I am used to reading lips just the way people really talk, so that is what is easiest for me to lip read.

Because I am hearing impaired, people often wonder if I can talk. Believe me, I can! In fact, sometimes my dad says I talk too much! My voice sounds a little different though. My friends say it sounds like I have a foreign accent. If you don't understand what I say, it's no big deal. Just ask me. But please include me in your conversation.

Sometimes when everybody is talking at once, I won't be able to lip read it all, and I will have to ask you what was said. *Please* don't say, "I'll tell you later," and then forget to do it. That drives me crazy! More than anything, just treat me like you would treat any other friend. I'd love to be friends with you.

325

Gena talking with the young authors who wrote this chapter

## Questions & Answers About Hearing Impairment

We found out many things about being hearing impaired by asking questions.

### What does it mean to be hearing impaired?

Some people believe that "hearing impaired" and "deaf" mean the same thing. Other people told us that when you are deaf you can't hear anything, but if you are hearing impaired you can hear something, although it might sound like just a whisper. In our book we have chosen to use the term hearing impaired because that is how Gena refers to herself.

Some people who are hearing impaired cannot understand spoken conversation without the help of a hearing aid. They may hear some sounds without the hearing aid, but these sounds are too faint to be understood.

There are many types and degrees of hearing loss. Try plugging your ears and having a friend whisper something to you. What you hear is kind of what it's like to have a hearing loss.

With other types of hearing loss, you can't hear certain frequencies. You might not hear the high tones of sounds or you might not hear the low tones. For example, you wouldn't hear all the notes of a song. Or in a conversation, you would hear silences where the tones you couldn't hear should be.

### How do you become hearing impaired?

You can become hearing impaired from many different things. Most commonly people are born with a hearing impairment. If a baby has a lot of ear infections, he or she might get a hearing impairment. A person might become hearing impaired by listening to very loud music or going to a rock concert and sitting too close to the loud speaker. Adults might get a hearing loss from operating noisy machines every day at their jobs. Many people lose their hearing naturally from old age.

### How long does it take to tell that a person is hearing impaired?

A person can be tested for a hearing loss in a short amount of time. If a baby is not learning to speak, does not react to loud noises, or doesn't seem to notice when someone calls his or her name, it might be a sign of hearing loss. Adults might find out later in life that they lost some of their hearing and not even know when it happened.

**Gena doing her homework**

Gena answering students' questions

### Do hearing impaired people ever get their hearing back?

Hearing impaired people usually do not get their hearing back and are hearing impaired their whole lives. There are some things that can be done to help hearing impaired people hear a little better. They might have surgery, or they might wear hearing aids to help make the sounds louder in their ears.

### Can hearing impaired people talk?

Hearing impaired people can talk, but it takes a lot of work to learn how. Imagine trying to learn another language without ever being able to hear someone say the words correctly. Hearing impaired people that do talk sound a little different from people who can hear. Some people sound like they have foreign accents, and some exaggerate the sounds in words.

Many hearing impaired people spend a lot of time with voice therapists who help them learn to speak by watching and touching.

A hearing impaired person can feel how words are sounded by touching their teacher's throat or their own throat while they talk. Some hearing impaired people choose not to talk and prefer to use sign language or another form of communication.

### What is sign language?

Sign language is a language made up of hand movements, gestures, and facial expressions. Each letter of the alphabet is signed in a different way. Just as Spanish and Japanese are complete languages, American Sign Language (ASL) is a language in itself, with thousands of signs for different words. There are many places where you can take a class and learn sign language. Check in your phone book under "Deaf" or "Hearing Impaired" to see what organizations are in your area.

### How do you talk to hearing impaired people?

If they can read lips, you talk to hearing impaired people just as you would to a hearing person. If the person cannot read lips, then you could spell out what you want to say using hand signs, act out what you want to say, learn American Sign Language, or write a note.

### What are some of the things that make life easier for hearing impaired people?

There are many things that help hearing impaired people. Many hearing impaired people have doorbells that flash a light instead of ringing when someone is at the door.

There are also phones that flash a light when the phone rings, and alarm clocks that light up instead of make noise.

To watch television, hearing impaired people use a system called closed captioning. A program that is closed captioned runs a special symbol on the screen to tell hearing impaired people they can use close captions. A special box called a decoder box prints the words spoken on the show at the bottom of the TV screen. This way a hearing impaired person can watch the show and read the words as they are spoken. We found out that as of 1993, new televisions have this decoder box built right inside the television. In fact, if you have a newer television, you could try this to see what it is like.

# GLOSSARY

Some of the words in this book may have pronunciations or meanings you do not know. This glossary can help you by telling you how to pronounce those words and by telling you the meanings with which those words are used in this book.

You can find out the correct pronunciation of any glossary word by using the special spelling after the word and the pronunciation key that runs across the bottom of the glossary pages.

The full pronunciation key opposite shows how to pronounce each consonant and vowel in a special spelling. The pronunciation key at the bottom of the glossary pages is a shortened form of the full key.

# Full Pronunciation Key

## Consonant Sounds

| | | | | | |
|---|---|---|---|---|---|
| b | **b**i**b**, ca**bb**age | kw | **ch**oir, **qu**ick | t | **t**igh**t**, stopp**ed** |
| ch | **ch**ur**ch**, sti**tch** | l | **l**id, need**l**e, ta**ll** | th | ba**th**, **th**in |
| d | **d**ee**d**, mail**ed**, | m | a**m**, **m**an, du**mb** | *th* | ba**th**e, **th**is |
| | pu**dd**le | n | **n**o, sudd**en** | v | ca**v**e, val**v**e, **v**ine |
| f | **f**ast, **f**i**f**e, o**ff**, | ng | thi**ng**, i**nk** | w | **w**ith, **w**olf |
| | **ph**rase, rou**gh** | p | **p**o**p**, ha**pp**y | y | **y**es, **y**olk, on**i**on |
| g | **g**a**g**, **g**et, fin**g**er | r | **r**oa**r**, **rh**yme | z | ro**s**e, si**z**e, |
| h | **h**at, **wh**o | s | mi**ss**, **s**au**c**e, **sc**ene, | | **x**ylophone, **z**ebra |
| hw | **wh**ich, **wh**ere | | **s**ee | zh | gara**g**e, plea**s**ure, |
| j | **j**ud**g**e, **g**em | sh | di**sh**, **sh**ip, **s**ugar, | | vi**s**ion |
| k | **c**at, **k**i**ck**, s**ch**ool | | ti**ss**ue | | |

## Vowel Sounds

| | | | | | |
|---|---|---|---|---|---|
| ă | r**a**t, l**au**gh | ŏ | h**o**rrible, p**o**t | û | c**ir**cle, f**ur**, h**ear**d, |
| ā | **a**pe, **ai**d, p**ay** | ō | g**o**, r**ow**, t**oe**, | | t**er**m, t**ur**n, **ur**ge, |
| â | **ai**r, c**a**re, w**ea**r | | th**ough** | | w**or**d |
| ä | f**a**ther, k**o**ala, y**a**rd | ô | **a**ll, c**au**ght, f**o**r, p**aw** | yōō | c**u**re |
| ĕ | p**e**t, pl**ea**sure, **a**ny | oi | b**oy**, n**oi**se, **oi**l | yŏŏ | ab**u**se, **u**se |
| ē | b**e**, b**ee**, **ea**sy, pian**o** | ou | c**ow**, **ou**t | ə | **a**bout, sil**e**nt, penc**i**l, |
| ĭ | **i**f, p**i**t, b**u**sy | ōō | f**u**ll, t**oo**k, w**o**lf | | lem**o**n, circ**u**s |
| ī | b**y**, p**ie**, h**igh** | ōō | b**oo**t, fr**ui**t, fl**ew** | | |
| î | d**ear**, d**eer**, f**ie**rce, | ŭ | c**u**t, fl**oo**d, r**ou**gh, | | |
| | m**e**re | | s**o**me | | |

## Stress Marks

Shown by accent marks **′** and ′ and by heavy, dark letters. **dic•tion•ar•y** (**dĭk**′shə nĕr′ē)

**backstop**

**am•bas•sa•dor** (ăm **băs'**ə dər) *n.* An official representative of a country sent by his or her government to another country: *The ambassador from China represents her government in the United States.*

**au•di•tion** (ô **dĭsh'**ən) *v.* To give a short performance testing ability as an actor: *Felita does audition for the leading role in the school play, but she doesn't get the part.*

**back•stop** (**băk'**stôp') *n.* A screen or fence behind the catcher that helps to keep a ball from being thrown or hit outside the playing field: *The umpire stood between the catcher and the backstop.*

**C**

**cast•ing** (**kăst'**ĭng) *n.* The selection of actors or performers: *When she finished the casting, the teacher announced the player for each part.*

**crouch** (krouch) *v.* To stoop low with bent legs; to squat: *Jake crouched by the wood stove and put another log on the fire.*

**E**

**es•ca•pade** (**ĕs'**kə pād') *n.* A carefree adventure that may have broken the rules: *The children left without asking permission, and they were afraid that they would get in trouble for their escapade.*

**F**

**for•eign** (**fôr'**ĭn) *adj.* From another country: *The foreign students in our class were from Germany and Spain.*

**for•eign•er** (**fôr'**ə nər) *n.* A person from another country: *The girl from China is a foreigner in the United States.*

**foul** (foul) *n.* In baseball, a ball that lands or is caught outside the field of play: *I thought I hit the ball straight, but it went outside third base and was a foul.* —*adj.* 1. Outside the field of play: *The foul ball went to the right of first base.* 2. Disgusting in taste, smell, or appearance: *The bananas I bought two weeks ago smell foul now.*

ă pat / ā pay / â care / ä father / ĕ pet / ē be / ĭ pit / ī ride / î fierce / ŏ pot / ō go
ô paw, for

**gasp** (găsp) v. To try to catch one's breath sharply: *Out of breath, Alex* **gasped** *when he tried to speak.*

**grap•ple** (**grăp'**əl) v. To struggle: *He* **grappled** *with his large winter coat as if he were wrestling with a person.*

**her•o•ine** (**hĕr'**ō ĭn) n. The most important female character: *The* **heroine,** *Priscilla, was the central character of the school play.*

**im•i•tate** (**ĭm'**ĭ tāt') v. To try to act, look, or sound like someone or something else: *Gigi* **imitated** *Paquito's laugh so well that even Paquito couldn't tell the difference.*

**play-off** (**plā'**ôf') or (**plā'**ŏf') n. Game or games played to determine the winner of a championship: *The team that wins two out of the three games of the* **play-offs** *will be the champion team.*

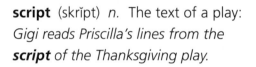

**re•cite** (rĭ **sīt'**) v. To repeat aloud for an audience, often from memory: *I have memorized a poem, and tomorrow I will* **recite** *it in front of the class.*

**rep•u•ta•tion** (rĕp'yə **tā'**shən) n. What people think and say the quality of someone or something is: *She is known for her good manners, and she lives up to her* **reputation.**

**script** (skrĭpt) n. The text of a play: *Gigi reads Priscilla's lines from the* **script** *of the Thanksgiving play.*

**series** (**sîr'**ēz) n. Several things or events that appear in a row or one after the other: *If the Elks beat the Hawks, they will play three games in a* **series** *against the Eagles.*

**squad** (skwŏd) n. A small group: *Our baseball team was a* **squad** *made up of twelve players.*

**swag•ger** (**swăg'**ər) v. To walk with a bold or proud manner: *The winners* **swaggered** *into the room, looking very pleased with themselves.*

oi **oi**l / o͞o b**oo**k / o͞o b**oo**t / ou **ou**t / ŭ **cu**t / û f**u**r / th ba**th** / *th* ba**the** / ə **a**go, it**e**m, penc**i**l, at**o**m, circ**u**s

Glossary 4

**thun•der** (**thŭn′**dər) *v.* 1. To make a loud noise: *He **thundered** into the room, banging his boots loudly on the wooden floor.* 2. To speak loudly: *"Get out of my way!" the man **thundered.***

ă pat / ā pay / â care / ä father / ĕ pet / ē be / ĭ pit / ī ride / î fierce / ŏ pot / ō go
ô paw, for

# ACKNOWLEDGMENTS

For each of the selections listed below, grateful acknowledgment is made for permission to excerpt and/or reprint original or copyrighted material, as follows:

## Selections

"China's Little Ambassador," from *In the Year of the Boar and Jackie Robinson,* by Bette Bao Lord. Copyright © 1984 by Bette Bao Lord. Reprinted by permission of HarperCollins Children's Books, a division of HarperCollins Publishers.

Selection from *Felita,* by Nicholasa Mohr. Copyright © 1979 by Nicholasa Mohr. Reprinted by permission of Dial Books for Young Readers, a division of Penguin USA.

"From the Not-So-Secret Files of the Bug Squad," from August/September,1993 *Zillions* magazine. Copyright © 1993 by Consumers Union of U.S., Inc., Yonkers, NY 10703–1057. Reprinted by permission.

Selection from *Hoang-Anh: A Vietnamese-American Boy,* by Diane Hoyt-Goldsmith. Copyright © 1992 by Diane Hoyt-Goldsmith. Reprinted by permission of Holiday House, Inc.

*Like Jake and Me,* by Mavis Jukes, illustrated by Lloyd Bloom. Text copyright © 1984 by Mavis Jukes. Illustrations copyright © 1984 by Lloyd Bloom. Reprinted by permission of Random House, Inc.

"Living with a Hearing Impairment," from *Kids Explore The Gifts of Children with Special Needs,* by Westridge Young Writers Workshop. Copyright © 1994 by John Muir Publications. Reprinted by permission.

*Magic Eye: A New Way of Looking at the World,* by N.E. Thing Enterprises. Copyright © 1993 by N.E. Thing Enterprises. Reprinted by permission of Andrews and McMeel. All rights reserved.

Selection from *Me, Mop, and the Moondance Kid,* by Walter Dean Myers. Copyright © 1988 by Walter Dean Myers. Reprinted by permission of Bantam Doubleday Dell Books for Young Readers.

## Poetry

"Ma! Don't Throw That Shirt Out!," from *The New Kid on the Block,* by Jack Prelutsky. Copyright © 1984 by Jack Prelutsky. Reprinted by permission of Greenwillow Books, a division of William Morrow & Company, Inc.

"Narcissa," from *Bronzeville Boys and Girls,* by Gwendolyn Brooks. Copyright © 1956 by Gwendolyn Brooks Blakely. Reprinted by permission of HarperCollins Publishers.

"Reflection," by Shel Silverstein, from *A Light in the Attic.* Copyright © 1981 by Evil Eye Music, Inc. Reprinted by permission of HarperCollins Publishers.

"We Could Be Friends," from *The Way Things Are and Other Poems,* by Myra Cohn Livingston. Copyright © 1974 by Myra Cohn Livingston. Reprinted by permission of Marian Reiner for the author.

## Additional Acknowledgments

Special thanks to the teacher whose student's composition appears in the Be a Writer feature for this theme: Kris Corskie, North Beach Elementary School, Seattle, Washington.

# CREDITS

**Illustration** **222–235** Winson Trang **242** David Fuller **248** Cheryl Taylor **249** Shel Silverstein **250–263** Lloyd Bloom **274–291** Anthony Woolridge **298–320** Kevin Beilfuss

**Assignment Photography** **Cover/Back cover** Tracey Wheeler (background) **Title page** Tracey Wheeler (background); Tony Scarpetta (inset) **214–215** Tracey Wheeler **216–217** Dave Desroches **236–237** Tony Scarpetta **238–239, 266–267** Banta Digital Group **292–293** John Craig **294–295** Tony Scarpetta **321** Quintin Wright **Back cover insets** Dave Desroches (tm); Tracey Wheeler (m, bm); Banta Digital Group (bl)

**Photography** **220** Courtesy of Betty Bao Lord **221** Courtesy of Winson Trang **238** Courtesy of Mark Aoyama **241** Courtesy of Mark Aoyama **242–47** © 1991 Lawrence Migdale (r) **264** Courtesy of Mavis Jukes **265** Courtesy of Lloyd Bloom **268** Courtesy of Kaiser-Porcelain (l); Mark R. Holmes (c) National Geographic Society **269** Courtesy of of Blue Mountain Arts **270** Rick Brown/Stock Boston **271** "Relativity" M.C. Escher/Art Resource (t) private collection; J. Eastcott/Y. Momatiuk/Stock Boston (b) **292** Courtesy of Walter Dean Myers **293** Courtesy of Anthony Woolridge **296** Flip Chalfant/The Image Bank **297** Tosca Radigonda/The Image Bank **321** Courtesy of Nicholasa Mohr(t) **322–323** David R. Frazier Photolibrary (b) **324–328** John Muir Publications **Glossary 3** Jim Zukerman/Westlight (tl)